A2 Physical Education
UNIT 4

Edexcel

Unit 4: Global Trends in International Sport

112 586

D1440222

Philip Allan Updates
Market Place
Deddington
Oxfordshire
OX15 0SE

tel: 01869 338652
fax: 01869 337590
e-mail: sales@philipallan.co.uk
www.philipallan.co.uk

© Philip Allan Updates 2005

ISBN-13: 978-1-84489-013-2
ISBN-10: 1-84489-013-9

All rights reserved; no part of this publication may be reproduced, stored in a retrieval system, or transmitted, in any form or by any means, electronic, mechanical, photocopying, recording or otherwise without either the prior written permission of Philip Allan Updates or a licence permitting restricted copying in the United Kingdom issued by the Copyright Licensing Agency Ltd, 90 Tottenham Court Road, London W1T 4LP.

This Guide has been written specifically to support students preparing for the Edexcel A2 Physical Education Unit 4 examination. The content has been neither approved nor endorsed by Edexcel and remains the sole responsibility of the author.

Printed by MPG Books, Bodmin

Environmental information
The paper on which this title is printed is sourced from managed, sustainable forests.

A2 Physical Education

Contents

Introduction

■ ■ ■

Content Guidance

■ ■ ■

Questions and Answers

Introduction

About this guide

This guide is written to help you prepare for the Unit 4 examination of the Edexcel A2 Physical Education course. It covers the content of the Unit 4 specification: **Global Trends in International Sport**. The specification for this unit is split into two sections, and this is reflected in the unit test. Section A is concerned with specific global cultures. You will be examined on one culture from this section, but you will need to study more than one in order to have choice in the test itself and to be able to develop comparisons between cultures to support your analysis of the synoptic issues in Section B. This guide covers the cultures of the USA and Australia. In Section B you will be required to answer essay questions comparing countries through the issues associated with global games, and you will need to draw on knowledge gained in your study of Units 1, 3, 4 and 6.

There are three sections to this guide:

- **Introduction** — this provides advice on how to use this guide, an explanation of the skills required to complete the unit successfully and guidance on revision and examination techniques.
- **Content Guidance** — this section gives a point-by-point description of all the basic facts you need to know and all the major concepts you need to understand for Unit 4. Although each fact and concept is explained where necessary, you must be prepared to use other resources to improve your understanding. The topics in this section correspond to those in the specification.
- **Questions and Answers** — this section provides examples of the sorts of questions you can expect to encounter in the unit test. It would be impossible to give examples of every kind of question in one book, but these should give you a good idea of what to expect. Each question has been attempted by two candidates, Candidate A and Candidate B. Their answers, along with examiner's comments, should help you to see what you need to do to score a high mark — and how you can easily drop marks, even though you may understand the subject matter.

What can I assume about the guide?

You can assume that:

- the topics described in the Content Guidance section correspond to those in the specification
- the basic facts you need to know are stated clearly
- the major concepts you need to understand are explained
- the questions at the end of the guide are similar in style to those that will appear in the unit examination

- the answers supplied are genuine answers — not concocted by the author
- the standard of marking is broadly equivalent to that which will be applied to your unit test answers

What can I *not* assume about the guide?

You must *not* assume that:
- every last detail has been covered
- the diagrams used will be the same as those used in the unit test
- the way in which the concepts are explained is the only way in which they can be presented in an examination
- the range of question types presented is exhaustive (examiners are always thinking of new ways to test a topic)

So how should I use this guide?

This guide lends itself to a number of uses throughout your physical education course — it is not *just* a revision aid. Because the Content Guidance is laid out in sections that correspond to those of the specification for Unit 4, you can use it:
- to check that your notes cover the material required by the specification
- to identify strengths and weaknesses
- as a reference for homework and internal tests
- during your revision to prepare 'bite-sized' chunks of related material, rather than being faced with a file full of notes

The Questions and Answers section can be used to:
- identify the terms used by examiners in questions and what these expect of you
- familiarise yourself with the style of questions you can expect
- identify the ways in which marks are lost as well as the ways in which they are gained

Preparing for the Unit 4 test

Preparation for examinations is a very personal thing. Different people prepare, equally successfully, in different ways. The key is being totally honest about what actually *works* for *you*. This is *not* necessarily the same as the style you would like to adopt. It is no use preparing to a background of loud music if this distracts you. Taking a sporting analogy, the practice environment should mirror the competitive one. The competitive environment is the examination room.

Whatever your style, you must have a revision plan. Sitting down the night before the examination with a file full of notes and a textbook does not constitute an effective plan — it is just desperation! Whatever your personal revision style is, there are a number of strategies you *must* adopt and others you *could* consider.

What you *must* do

- Leave yourself enough time to *cover* all the material identified in the Unit 4 specification.
- Make sure that you actually have all the material to hand (use this book as a basis).
- Identify weaknesses early in your preparation so that you have time to do something about them.
- Familiarise yourself with the terminology used in the examination questions.
- Remember to read though your notes and revision points from Units 2 and 3 of the AS course.

What you *could* do

- Copy selected sections of your notes.
- Summarise your notes into a more compact format, including the key points.
- Create your own flash cards — write key points on postcards (carry them round with you for a quick revise during a coffee break or on the bus).
- Make audio recordings of your notes and/or the key points and play these back.
- Make a PowerPoint presentation of the key points and use this to revise in the last few days before the unit test.
- Discuss a topic with a friend also studying the same course.
- Try to explain a topic to someone *not* following the course.
- Practise examination questions on the topic — particularly planning essay answers.

Approaching the Unit 4 test

Terms used in examination questions

You will be asked precise questions in the examination, so you can save a lot of valuable time — as well as ensuring you score as many marks as possible — by knowing what is expected. Terms most commonly used are explained below.

Brief

This means that only a short statement of the main points is required.

Define

This requires you to state the meaning of a term, without using the term itself.

Describe

This is a request for factual detail about a structure or process, expressed logically and concisely, without explanation.

Discuss

You are required to give a critical account of various viewpoints and arguments on the topic set, drawing attention to their relative importance and significance.

Evaluate

This means that a judgement of evidence and/or arguments is required.

Explain

This means that reasons have to be included in your answer.

Identify

This requires a word, phrase or brief statement to show that you recognise a concept or theory in an item.

List

This requires a sequence of numbered points, one below the other, with no further explanation.

Outline

This means give only the main points, i.e. don't go into detail. Don't be tempted to write more than necessary — this will waste time.

State

A brief, concise answer, without reasons, is required.

Suggest

This means that the question has no fixed answer and a wide range of reasonable responses is acceptable.

What is meant by...?

This usually requires a definition. The amount of information needed is indicated by the mark allocation.

When you finally open the test paper, it can be quite a stressful moment. You may not recognise the diagram or quote used in Question 1. It can be quite demoralising to attempt a question at the start of an examination if you are not feeling very confident about it. However, remember that you have a lot of choice. Read all the questions carefully before deciding which to attempt. Other strategies for the examination itself include the following:

- *Do not* begin to write as soon as you open the paper.
- *Do not* necessarily answer Question 1 first (the examiner did not sequence the questions with your particular favourites in mind).
- *Do* scan *all* the questions on the paper before you start your answers.
- *Do* identify those questions about which you feel most confident.
- *Do* answer *first* those questions about which you feel most confident, regardless of their order in the paper.
- *Do remember* that the essay question in section C scores double and you should, therefore, take more time planning and writing your answer to this part of the paper.
- *Do read* the question carefully — if you are asked to explain, then explain, don't just describe.
- *Do* take notice of the mark allocation and try to match this to the number of points you make in your answer.

- *Do* try to stick to the point in your answer (it is easy to stray into related areas that will not score marks and use up valuable time).
- *Make sure* you fulfil the examination rubric, i.e. answer the correct number of questions from the right sections.

Effective essay writing

The term synoptic refers to an overview of knowledge. In order to answer any synoptic question you should refer to a multitude of topic areas. The main theme for synoptic questions is 'global games' and you will need to refer to a range of examples from various global games in your answer.

The Unit 4 synoptic section has a scientific emphasis.

A good essay will:
- have a clear, recorded plan (which must be flexible and answer the question)
- be at least two sides in length and contain seven or eight paragraphs
- have an introduction that provides an overview of the essay content
- define terms
- work through the question in an identifiable order (e.g. chronologically, with examples in a logical order)
- refer to different global games and not just be a reproduction of an AS Olympic essay
- be analytical and challenge ideas with substantiated argument
- have a conclusion that sums up the answer
- have answered the question

A poor essay will:
- contain the question written out again
- not have a plan
- be written in bullet points
- guess at facts, figures and dates
- have dates out of sequence
- reproduce or regurgitate a premeditated essay plan
- argue a point rather than remaining neutral

In the exam

Read the questions *carefully* — at least twice — to ensure that you understand fully what each question is asking. Plan your time and stick to it. Aim to spend at least 35 minutes writing your essay.

Content
Guidance

This section is a guide to the content of **Unit 4: Global Trends in International Sport**. The main areas of this unit are:

- The background and historical development of sport in the USA
- Mass participation and elite sport in the USA
- The background and historical development of sport in Australia
- Mass participation and elite sport in Australia
- Synoptic topics

You may already be familiar with some of the information in these topic areas. However, it is important that you know and understand this information exactly as described in the specification. This summary of the specification content highlights key points. Therefore, you should find it useful when revising for the Unit 4 test.

The USA and Australia have been chosen as the case studies because these are the most popular cultures with students.

The USA

Background and historical development of sport

Key points

- The mainstream social values present in the USA and the factors that are responsible for their prevalence within US culture.
- Definitions and applications of the three main sporting ethics in the USA — the Lombardian ethic, the radical ethic and the counter-culture ethic (sometimes referred to as the recreational ethic).
- The concept of 'frontier spirit' and its relevance to the sports scene in the USA.
- The environmental and topographical factors that shape sport in the USA.

Geography and demography

- The population of the USA is 270 million, of which 80% are Caucasian.
- The USA is made up of 50 states that function and are administered with a degree of independence.
- There are extreme variations in topography — there is every type of terrain and climate in ten climatic zones. This can have a beneficial effect on sport and recreation.
- There is a huge spread between urban sprawls and true wilderness. However, the USA is a country with sophisticated communications.
- Three-quarters of the population live in cities, which favours spectator sports.
- The standard of living is among the highest in the world. This gives Americans more time for recreation than the inhabitants of other countries.
- Pride in the beauty and variety of the states and their natural environment is reflected in the so-called **frontier spirit**. This perhaps makes up for a lack of tradition and heritage. Most of US history is closely linked to the great outdoors and most of its modern-day population yearns to get back to nature. In some ways, this explains the popularity of summer camps for young people.
- Reflecting the decentralised administration of the country, there are both national and state parks.

Historical development

Modern US society grew from a string of British settlements on the east coast.

The War of Independence severed links with Europe and from this point US sport reflected the emergence of an American identity. The pioneering spirit of migration westwards during the nineteenth century is an important part of an underlying national character. Many of the sports played in the USA are adaptations of sports that originated in Britain and Europe at the start of the nineteenth century. However, many of the US versions were altered to reflect the New World status of the colonies and are now very much isolated in terms of competition. For example, rugby was adapted into American football, the current world championships of which only include American teams.

Social values and sporting ethics

US society is described as egalitarian, pluralistic and multicultural. These concepts underpin a traditional value system, based on a work ethic in which each individual is free to compete with others. This leads to the philosophy of **meritocracy**, which states that individuals who work hard should be rewarded with symbols of success such as money, fame and power. In sport, a strong emphasis on winning can be seen as a clear reflection of the underlying value system of the USA.

Sport and the **American Dream** are central elements of American culture. Sports talk, images and personalities are found in all areas of American life. The pursuit of the American Dream of achievement, mobility and success is a major driving force for most Americans and is clearly reflected in the US sports scene.

The win-at-all-costs ethic (**Lombardian ethic**) is clearly evident throughout sport in America. This is encouraged by the philosophy of the frontier spirit, in which the emphasis is on the survival of the fittest or toughest. American sports are high scoring and action packed to maximise their entertainment value.

American sport is extremely commercial. Sport at every level, from high school to professional league, is run as a business. The media have a great deal of influence and most American sport relies on funds generated by television deals and advertising. The aforementioned philosophy of meritocracy — in which people are paid in accordance with their level of work or talents — coupled with the amounts of money raised through commercial venture, results in American sports stars being the richest in the world.

What the examiners will expect you to be able to do

- Identify and discuss the mainstream social values and be able to explain the factors responsible for their creation.
- Identify and describe the ethics present in sport in the USA.
- Discuss the environmental and topographical factors that influence sport in the USA.
- Chart the historical development of physical education and sport in the USA.
- Define and explain the term 'frontier spirit' as well as applying the ethic to the sports scene in the USA.

Tip The 'win ethic' is so prevalent in both life and sport in the USA that you can probably use it in most of your examination answers. Remember that it can also be referred to as the Lombardian ethic or the win-at-all-costs ethic. Credit will only be given once for using any of these terms.

Mass participation and elite sport

This part of the specification covers:

- the attitude towards, and structure of, PE and extracurricular sport in US high schools
- the structure of sport within higher education, covering both intercollegiate and intramural sport
- the sports scholarship and how the education sector acts as a nursery for elite sport in the USA
- the structure and commercial nature of professional sport
- the role of the media and status of professional sport
- the role of sporting participation, with a focus on community sport and sport for the young (Little League)
- the role of the national parks and their links to alternative and wilderness sports

Sporting participation in the USA

- The USA has evolved a different sports club system from that in Europe. Sport tends to be based on high school, college and professional levels. There is only limited opportunity outside these to participate in sport. Public parks and open spaces do offer the chance to take part in some physical recreation, but there is little public-sector provision.
- America supports the concept of lifetime sport. In many areas, sports competitions are organised for older citizens (e.g. the Golden Olympics).
- The main route into elite sport in the USA is through the education system. The pathway is summarised in the diagram below.

'Big four' professional leagues

Draft

College teams (National Collegiate Athletic Association)

High-school teams

It is accepted that successful high-school students will receive **athletic scholarships**. An athletic scholarship is a grant-in-aid to help cover tuition fees and board.

School and college sport

In the field of school and college sport, the USA is unique. In many areas where there is no professional franchise, high school and college teams are substitutes for professional sport and attract a huge community following.

The revenue-making sports are football and basketball, with most college football games attracting over 50 000 paying spectators. Even high school teams attract crowds in the thousands. The money made from gate receipts is used to ensure that teams attract the best players, as well as providing full-time coaches and state-of-the-art equipment.

Further funding comes from television rights and alumni organisations (often referred to as 'booster clubs') that raise money for the teams. Just as with the professional teams, it is important for college teams to be successful. To ensure this, they recruit talented athletes from high schools nationwide, who are offered scholarships to attend college.

Professional sport

- The professional sports scene is dominated by the big four — basketball, baseball, American football and ice hockey. All attract considerable public support and commercial backing.
- All sports in the USA are administered by a number of decentralised autonomous governing bodies, with little interference or support from state or federal governments.

Little League

Little League is a sports programme aimed at young Americans. Club-based leagues for children are run in a number of sports — for example, Pop Warner Football, Biddy Basketball and Pee Wee Baseball. The teams are run by parents and compete in structured leagues that mirror the professional leagues, with conferences, play-offs and super bowls. Little League Baseball has a rival world series competition, which is shown live on television.

Wilderness sport

The USA has a large range of National Parks, which are easily accessible and well managed, providing recreational opportunities for all Americans.

Over the last 30 years, there has been a great upsurge in the popularity of outback sports such as canoeing, mountain biking and snow boarding, fuelled by a desire to:
- return to the concept of the frontier spirit that was so important to the pioneers who founded America
- escape from the 'rat race' and the urbanisation of modern living

This is an example of the new counter-culture movement — some Americans are seeking alternative leisure pursuits that do not have trappings of elitism and commercialism and are not win driven.

What the examiners will expect you to be able to do

- Describe the structure of sport and physical education in schools and colleges.
- Chart the historical development of professional sport in the USA.

- Describe the structure and commercial nature of professional sport in the USA.
- Explain the role of sporting participation in the USA.
- Describe the structure and scope of Little League sport.

Tip Remember that America has a decentralised society with separate state influence. Sport in America reflects this, with autonomous sports leagues and domination by the private sector.

Australia

Background and historical development of sport

Key points

- The mainstream social values present in Australia and the factors that are responsible for their prevalence within Australian culture.
- The culture and sports of the indigenous population (Aboriginals).
- How the development of sport in Australia reflects its colonial history and how it has matured to reflect the new Australian identity and values.
- State and federal policies in relation to games and sports.
- The use of sport as a vehicle for nation building and shop-window profiling.
- The environmental, political and topographical factors that shape sport in Australia.

Geography, demography and administration

- Relative to its small population, Australia enjoys an extraordinary degree of sporting success. The population of around 18 million has a young profile with nearly half of the current population aged under 30.
- Australia is the only nation that occupies a whole continent and its flora and fauna are unique. However, Australia is also a culture of contradictions. It has a huge land mass covering almost 3 million square miles but has one of the most urbanised populations, with 85% of people living in only 3.3% of the land area.
- Most of the population lives on the low-lying coastal plains running round the south and east coasts, so the accessibility of the beach and sea influences the leisure activities Australians choose.
- Australia consists of a number of self-governing states and two areas that have territorial status.
- The country is governed under a federal system similar to the one that operates in the USA, the main difference being that Australia has Commonwealth status and consequently Queen Elizabeth II is still its head of state.

- The system of administration is decentralised. The role of the federal government in Canberra is to oversee national policies, administer the two territories, manage the economy and coordinate international affairs.

Tip Remember that although Australia is a decentralised society with separate state influence, Australian sport is, in the main, centrally organised, with the Australian Sports Commission taking a central role in the control and funding of sport.

Historical development

The native inhabitants of Australia — the Aboriginal people — are one of the oldest civilisations in the world. Originally, the Aboriginal people were nomadic hunter gatherers; the sport and recreation they practised was mainly functional and therefore helped refine hunting and survival skills. They remained isolated until the eighteenth century when European settlers discovered *Terra Australis* (sometimes referred to as the Great South Land).

In 1788, a British settlement was established in Port Jackson, the site of modern-day Sydney. Until the American War of Independence, Britain had sent convicts to America. American independence ended this practice and British prisons were overcrowded. This resulted increasingly in convicts being sent to Australia. Free settlements were also established in South Australia and Victoria and these underwent spectacular growth between 1870 and 1918. Sports popular in Britain were exported to Australia and adapted (e.g. Australian Rules Football).

After the First World War, Britain's hold on the colonies began to dwindle. The Balfour declaration of 1926 and the Statute of Westminster 1931 ceded control of the colonies and led to the recognition of Australia's states as governments in their own right. All states remained members of the reformed Commonwealth.

Although a young country, Australia has used its colonial history to develop and foster high culture, though it is true to say that sport dominates most Australian households. Younger members of the population tend to participate in a range of sports; older members generally spectate and help organise and administer sport.

Australian homes are often well endowed with indoor and outdoor space. Therefore, home-based recreations around the pool and 'barbie' are very popular.

A degree of the old independence of the states is reflected in sport, with different styles of football enjoying popularity in different states. Australian Rules football is the dominant game in Victoria and South Australia; rugby is more popular in New South Wales and Queensland.

There has been a high level of government investment in sport. The administration and organisation of sport and recreation in Australia follows this pattern, with each state or territory having a department responsible for sport and recreation and its own elite academy. However, there is also a powerful centralising effect from the federally funded Australian Sports Commission and its Institute network.

The Australian Government has made a concerted effort to fund and promote sport in Australia, both in terms of elite national squads and sport for all. It believes in the power of sport as a vehicle for nation building and shop-window profiling.

What the examiners will expect you to be able to do

- Identify and discuss the mainstream social values in Australia and be able to explain the factors responsible for their creation.
- Discuss the environmental and topographical factors that influence sport in Australia.
- Chart the historical development of physical education and sport in Australia.
- Explain how the Australians use sport as a vehicle for nation building.

Mass participation and elite sport

This part of the specification covers:

- the historical development of physical education within Australian schools and colleges
- the attitude towards, and the structure of, PE and extracurricular sport in Australian high schools, including the concept of the Sport Education in Physical Education Program (SEPEP)
- the structure of sport within higher education, covering both intercollegiate and intramural sport
- the historical development of professional sport
- the structure and commercial nature of professional sport in Australia
- the structure and role of the Australian Institute of Sport
- the role of sporting participation with a focus on community sport (Active Australia) and sport for the young (Aussie Sport)
- the role of the national parks and their links to alternative and wilderness sports in Australia

National Parks and wilderness sports

Australia is blessed with vast areas of wilderness and regions of outstanding beauty. There is a large number of national parks, both at federal and state level, all offering the chance for Australians to discover the 'outback'. Australians have a tradition of outdoor recreation, and recent developments in transport and equipment, together with an increase in the standard of living, mean that most people can participate in a range of wilderness sports.

Sporting participation

Australia has a centralised sports system in a decentralised society. However, the Australian Sports Commission (ASC) has developed a well-thought-out participation pyramid, which does seem to ensure success both in terms of promoting sports participation and developing successful elite performers.

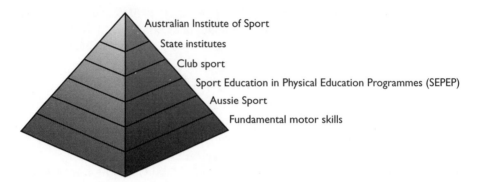

According to census data in 2000, 90% of Australians participate in sport — environmental and cultural factors facilitate access to recreation. The Active Australia programme coordinated by the ASC has the slogan 'From six to sixty', which gives a clear message that both young and old should be involved in some level of physical activity.

In 1986, the ASC launched a national programme (Aussie Sport) aimed at introducing sport to young people. This programme was offered by schools, clubs and other community groups and dominated the sports education of young people. It allowed children to develop skills, promoted fun and enjoyment, encouraged everyone to participate and highlighted the importance of fair play.

Sport and physical education in Australian schools

What does a typical Australian Year 10 student do in PE and sport at school?

Compulsory studies
- PE occupies 100 minutes per week.
- Sport Education occupies 100 minutes per week.

Students can:
- follow a multi-activity model in which the teacher leads 5–6 week units of various sports using a skills/practice/games type approach

or

- experience activities and sports through the new SEPEP curriculum model in which they are empowered to run most aspects of their own sports season. They take on the roles of coach, captain, referee, player, statistician, sports journalist, first aider, administrator and so on. The teacher assumes the role of facilitator (national coach) and works on a one-to-one basis with students along the skill continuum.

Elective studies
- Elective PE is a mixture of practical and theory, which occupies 150 minutes per week. It covers similar topics to AS/A2 PE but at a lower level.
- Regular inter-school sport teams practice occupies an hour per week. The sports vary according to season.

THE HENLEY COLLEGE LIBRARY

content guidance

- Specialist sport teams in soccer and volleyball have qualified teachers/coaches that prepare them for state and national competitions. Ninety minutes are allocated to this.

On top of this, students are released from their academic classes to pursue sport in other ways. For instance, all interschool sporting teams in government schools play fixtures during the school day — not after school, as in the private school system. If successful, this could mean up to four days out of a school term providing the team keeps winning. The structure is set up as shown in the following example from Ballarat Secondary School's Sports Association (BSSSA):

Government of Victoria School Sports — The Pathway	
Stage	**Competition**
1	Intra-college selection is often done on a house or form basis at lunch times and is used for selection of interschool teams.
2	Local association sport involves a round robin competition against six other government schools in the following sports: Term 1: tennis/cricket/softball(G)/baseball(B)/volleyball/athletics/swimming Term 2: Australian rules football/soccer/netball/hockey Term 3: basketball/table tennis/squash/badminton Term 4: alternative/modified sports (Super 8s cricket/triathlon/touch rugby/beach volleyball)
3	At the country zone level, the school team that wins its sport at stage 2 represents its local association against others in the region. For example, this would involve the western half of Victoria and include the Ballarat, Geelong, Colac and Wimmera Associations. It involves extensive travel to play schools that may be 300 km away. Our zone is called the Western Zone country.
4	The Western Zone country winner plays the Metropolitan winner to determine the Western Zone representative. This involves playing against schools from the western suburbs of Melbourne, such as Essendon, Footscray and Werribee. It is often the first time that students from country areas experience first hand the multiculturalism that exists in Australia. Ethnic groups tend to be confined to large cities rather than rural areas, although this is changing with the improvement of roads and transport.
5	The winner of the Western Zone final earns the right to play in the Victoria Secondary Schools Sports Association state final in that sport. For example, we would play for the Western Zone against schools which have won their way through to represent Southern, Eastern and Northern Zones. At this level, you play against schools from all over the state.

A significant number of students are also involved in one or more community sports where they are required to train twice a week and to commit to competitions at the weekends.

Other opportunities

- **Sports leader's certificate** — this can be achieved by coaching a variety of sports in local primary schools and running culminating events involving several of these schools. The certificate may be worked towards both during school hours and after school.

- **Sports persons in schools days** — athletes on Victorian Institute of Sport scholarships visit schools and run clinics and come-and-try days. This is part of the contractual obligations of the elite athlete and there is no cost to the school or the students.
- **State sporting association visits** — the state sporting associations send a Development Officer to schools to run clinics at no charge to schools or students. After the clinics, the Development Officer usually arranges a tournament between schools, with the winning school playing at a prestigious venue. For example, the final of the Victoria Cricket Association Super 8s Competition is played on the Melbourne Cricket Ground.

Elite sport

Failure at the Montreal Olympics in 1976 led to a major review of the sports system and a push to make Australian sport great through a number of initiatives: Aussie Sport, Active Australia, Sports Search, the Australian Institute of Sport and state academies.

Australian Institute of Sport (AIS)

The objectives of the AIS are:

- to enhance the sporting performances of Australia's elite and potentially elite athletes and teams
- to enhance the personal, educational and vocational development opportunities for elite athletes
- to improve the efficiency and effectiveness of the national-level sporting agencies in their management of Australian sport

The AIS is possibly the best centre for elite athlete preparation in the world. No expense is spared in providing Australia's top performers with the best backup and support. Funding is mainly federal, with some commercial sponsorship. The AIS and its satellite institutes in each state have created an effective production line of elite performers who have put Australia at the top level of global sport. Athletes receive scholarships to attend the AIS; there are 600 full-time and 270 visiting scholarships available each year.

Each state has its own elite academy, though there have been some attempts to centralise these. The executive officers of each academy meet as the National Elite Sports Council.

Professional sport

Professional sport still tends to follow a British style model, with autonomous clubs and governing bodies. However, there is an increasing American influence with the emergence of Super League in rugby league and the Australian Football League, as well as drafts in Aussie rules and rugby league. This is where the best young players from the junior leagues are ranked in terms of ability and then contracted to professional teams.

What the examiners will expect you to be able to do

- Describe the structure and historical development of sport and physical education in Australian schools and colleges.
- Chart the historical development of professional sport in Australia.
- Describe the structure and commercial nature of professional sport in Australia.
- Explain the role of sporting participation in Australia.
- Describe the structure and scope of the Active Australia programme.
- Explain the structure of the AIS.
- Explain the rise of adventure and wilderness sports.

Synoptic issues

Sport as a show of national identity

The benefits of sporting success

The benefits of success in global sport for a country can be internal or external, economic or social.

Recorded benefits include:
- increased levels of tourism
- increased levels of commercial activity and employment
- improved health of the population
- greater social integration within society
- reductions in crime and anti-social behaviour

Global games as a shop window

The 'shop window' in sport is a market place in which a nation displays its sporting talent and in doing so gains publicity for itself. For smaller nations and those with little other global impact, success in international sport is a very important vehicle of self-promotion.

Global games receive widespread coverage on media networks and thus attract huge audiences. This creates a world stage and is the reason why individuals, groups and governments have used global games as a platform for propaganda. The 2004 Olympic Games attracted a global television audience of 4 billion while the 2002 World Cup final between Germany and Brazil attracted a television audience of 1 billion. This illustrates the high profile of global games.

Government influence and policy

Government influence and policy can change depending on how the particular government views the importance of sport. There are two extremes of influence:
- centralised — total control of the organisation and funding of sport
- decentralised — no central control of sport

Government influence may also fall between these extremes. Examples of different degrees of influence are shown in the table below.

Type/degree of government influence	Description	Example
Direct/central	• Complete control by central government • Total state funding	China
Indirect	• Indirect funding through programmes such as national lotteries • State plans to promote grass roots and elite sport	Spain
Limited	• Funding for grass root and Olympic teams	Finland
Minimal	• Funding for Olympic teams only • No state control of sport • Autonomy of sports bodies	USA

Systematic approach to preparation

The move from the recreational ethic in global sport to the win ethic is associated with a move towards highly structured and sophisticated programmes of development for elite sports teams and performers. The recreational ethic in global sport is based on the philosophy that sport is about taking part rather than winning.

East Germany was a country with a population of only 16 million and yet it managed to be in the top three for sports such as athletics, swimming and boxing. The whole sports system of this communist country was geared to selecting and developing champion performers. However, this was at the expense of the rest of the population.

By the 1970s, the rise in both the playing standards and the rewards (political and financial) available in global sport led to all cultures reassessing their approach to supporting elite performers. France became the first 'western' culture to adopt an Eastern-bloc-type centralised approach to elite sport, setting up a National Sports Institute (INSEP). Australia quickly followed by establishing the Australian Institute of Sport (AIS) in 1981.

Most cultures have now adopted a centralised approach to sports, based around national centres of excellence.

The systematic preparation of elite athletes
The way in which nations prepare elite athletes for global competition is becoming a complex and sophisticated business. Most nations have adopted the elitist model,

which was pioneered by the East Germans in the 1950s. The emphasis is on a few highly talented performers and the rest of the sports pyramid is largely ignored.

Use of global games for protest

Sport is very popular around the world and major events like the Olympic Games and the football World Cup are televised in every country. This is why such events have been the focus for political demonstration. Any person or country that wants to make a point is guaranteed maximum exposure at these events.

Examples of protests

1936 Olympic Games, Berlin

These were called the 'Nazi Olympics'. They were the first Olympic Games at which politics were openly evident. Hitler believed in the supremacy of the Aryan race ('true' Germans — blond-haired, blue-eyed and muscular) and that they would dominate the Games and show that the German race was superior to all others.

1968 Olympic Games, Mexico City

Two young black American athletes used the medal ceremony to show their support for the Black Power movement. As they stood on the medal podium listening to the American national anthem, they bowed their heads and each raised one gloved hand in the Black Power salute.

1972 Olympic Games, Munich: the terrorist games

During the games, Palestinian terrorists stormed part of the Olympic village, killed two members of the Israeli team and took nine more Israeli athletes as hostages. The German police attempted to stage a dramatic rescue but this went wrong, ending in the deaths of the nine athletes, a policeman and five terrorists.

1976 Olympic Games, Montreal

These games were boycotted by 25 African countries. (A boycott in sport is refusing to compete in an event, usually for political reasons.) This happened because New Zealand had been allowed to compete in the games, even though its rugby team had played against South Africa, which at the time was racially segregated.

1977 Gleneagles Agreement

This was an agreement among Commonwealth countries to sever sporting links with South Africa in response to the continued policy of apartheid practised by the South African government. Apartheid policies discriminated against black people in all levels of society, including sport.

1980 Olympic Games, Moscow

Boycotts dominated these games. In December 1979, the Soviet Union had invaded Afghanistan. To show that they did not agree with this, many countries did not take part in these Olympics, including the USA, Canada, West Germany, Japan and Kenya.

1984 Olympic Games, Los Angeles: tit-for-tat

Because the USA had led the boycott of the Moscow Olympics in 1980, the Soviet Union led a boycott of the 1984 games. No eastern bloc countries competed.

Political propaganda

Sport has long been used as a means of proving that one political system is better than another. Part of international sport is that different countries and systems compete against each other.

During the 1960s, 1970s and 1980s, the USA and the USSR spent huge amounts of money trying to outdo each other in sport. A win at the Olympics, it was said, proved that one political system (capitalism or communism) was better than the other. Countries also boycotted particular Olympics and used their power and influence to persuade other countries not to take part.

Countries can use sport to show their feelings by boycotting events or by persuading international sports organisations to ban a particular country from competition. Reasons include human rights violations. Human rights are basic entitlements and opportunities that all people should have. Issues about human rights have brought politics and sport together. In some countries, certain types of people have been denied these rights — for example, black people under the apartheid regime of South Africa. Apartheid was abolished in the 1990s.

Many sportspeople state that politics and sports should not mix. However, it is difficult for them not to when so many governments actively support and fund sports organisations in their countries.

For many, representing their nation is a huge achievement and one they can be proud of. They will be motivated by hearing the national anthem of their country and seeing that country's flag raised, as they stand on the winner's podium. It could be suggested that this too reflects political propaganda.

What the examiners will expect you to be able to do

- Discuss how sporting success can benefit a country internally and externally.
- Explain how governments can influence sport within a country.
- Describe examples of systematic preparation for sporting success.
- Discuss using global games to make protests.

Links

This topic is also covered in Unit 1.

The pursuit of global excellence

This section of the specification covers:

- systems of nurturing sports talents including similarities and differences between countries and the geographical and cultural factors that shape these systems

- how the East German model has been adopted and adapted in many countries
- an explanation, using examples from different cultures, of how nations use academies and sports schools to develop potential athletes
- how elite athletes are funded and supported
- the application of sports science through different training regimes
- the role of drugs and medicines in global sport
- geographical and cultural influences

The nurturing of sports talents

Excellence in sport
Excellence in sport has two meanings:
- **elitism**, which means 'all for the best — forget the rest'; all resources are focused on top performers
- **optimum performance**, which means that everyone has the chance to succeed

The elitist approach
Most societies emphasise elitism because this produces champions, and champions can be used as a 'shop window'.

There are three major stages in the development of excellence:
- selection
- development
- support

In the run up to the 1936 Berlin Olympics, Hitler had pioneered an approach using training camps and coaching in an attempt to ensure Aryan supremacy at the games. After the Second World War, the Eastern bloc countries were the first to develop a systematic approach to nurturing elite sports talent.

The Eastern bloc approach focused on the early identification of talent — often as early as primary school. This was then followed by full-time specialist training by professional coaches, which was funded by state governments. In the final phase of preparation, the best athletes would live and train at specialist centres of sports excellence, known as institutes. The system was extremely successful, though recent revelations of widespread drug abuse has somewhat tarnished this model of sports excellence.

The best example of this elitist approach to sports excellence was seen in East Germany, a country with a population of only 16 million that managed to be in the top three for sports such as athletics, swimming and boxing. The whole sports system of this communist country was geared to selecting and developing champion performers. However, this was at the expense of the rest of the population. The process began with every child in the education system being screened for sporting potential. At first, this involved gross motor skills but later more specific skill-based, physiological and psychological tests were used to identify talent and channel it into the appropriate sports. After selection, students were filtered up the sports pyramid through city sports schools, regional boarding schools and — the ultimate aim — the national training centre.

Western cultures

In Western cultures, the historical divide between amateurism and professionalism delayed any sustained approach to elite sports development. For most of the twentieth century, Olympic sports had to rely on the voluntary sector raising money through donations and fundraising events. Schools and universities took a central role in identifying and developing talented sports performers.

By the 1970s, the rise in both the playing standards and the rewards (political and financial) available in global sport led to all cultures reassessing their approach to supporting elite performers. France became the first 'western' culture to adopt an Eastern bloc-type centralised approach to elite sport by setting up a National Sports Institute (INSEP); Australia quickly followed by establishing the Australian Institute of Sport (AIS) in 1981.

The USA

In the USA, an alternative system of nurturing sports talent has emerged, based around the college scholarship system. This enables performers to train full time, using the excellent sports facilities offered by all colleges, and to receive athletic scholarships so that their amateur status is not affected.

Resulting models of nurturing talent

Consequently, by the 1980s, there were two main models for nurturing talent:
- a centralised model in which athletes received state scholarships
- a USA-style university model in which athletes received athletic scholarships

Both of these models were given the label 'shamateurism', as they were seen to abuse the concept of an amateur athlete.

The UK has relied heavily on the voluntary sector to support and finance its elite athletes. The UK is now unique in that most of its Olympic athletes receive no direct funding from the government. Before the change in the rules regarding amateur status, the Sports Aid Foundation provided most of the limited grants available for elite athletes in the UK. Since the end of the 1990s, this role has been taken on by the National Lottery through the Sports Lottery Fund, which is distributed by UK Sport.

Most cultures have now adopted a centralised approach based around national centres of excellence. The benefits of such an approach include:
- bringing together the best coaches
- making available the best possible facilities
- allowing performers to concentrate on full-time training
- creating an atmosphere of excellence
- allowing the transfer of knowledge, as well as skills and training methods, between different sports
- providing a more efficient method of directing funds

What the examiners will expect you to be able to do

- Discuss the various systems of nurturing sports talent.
- Explain how the East German model of sports excellence has been adopted and adapted in many countries.
- Explain how nations fund and support elite athletes.

Ethics and deviance in global sport

Key points

- Reasons for, and types of, deviance in global sport.
- The increasing commercialisation of global sport and its effect on deviance.
- The rise and fall of sporting ethics and the role of the international sports bodies in combating cheating.

The rise and fall of ethics in global sport

Sportsmanship is competing according to the spirit of fair play and within the rules and etiquette (unwritten rules) of the game or event.

Gamesmanship involves the use of unfair practices to gain an advantage, often against the rules and etiquette of the game or event.

Media coverage and commercialism may be contributing factors to increased levels of deviance in global sport. The rewards of winning are massive and there are many pressures to win at all costs.

Winning a gold medal is mandatory from a marketing perspective. There is little commercial value in winning silver or bronze. In elite sport, a fraction of a second or a few millimetres could mean financial security for life. It is suggested that this desire to win has led to a decline in sporting ethics. However, it is open to debate whether there is more cheating in modern-day sport. It may be that because sport is now more media focused, with reporters and television cameras at every international sporting event, we have become more informed.

Deviance

All sports have rules. **Deviance** occurs when participants break these rules. This is called **cheating** and it is an important issue in modern sport.

Cheating is not a new concept — the ancient Olympians took tonics to try to improve their performances. Some people would argue that cheating is an important element in sport and that without it sport would be dull.

Deviance is defined as any behaviour designed to gain unfair advantage by means of:

- gamesmanship
- deliberate infringement of rules
- interfering with equipment

- knowingly taking banned substances for the purpose of gaining unfair advantage
- being involved in an act, the prime purpose of which is to gain an unfair advantage over one's opponent

Deviance in sport is no longer limited to elite able-bodied sport. At almost every level, some individuals and teams feel a need to bend or break the rules in order to ensure victory. After the 2000 Paralympics, the Spanish Paralympic basketball team was ordered to return its gold medals after nearly all the players were found to have no disability. The Spanish authorities were so keen to bring home medals to ensure further funding that they openly manipulated registration of the basketball team to allow able-bodied players to participate.

Drugs in sport

During the last few years, drug abuse has been one of the main areas of deviance in sport. It is not clear whether the level of drug taking has increased or whether we are simply more aware of it because of improved testing systems. It is also very difficult to decide where the line should be drawn between illegal and legal substances — many athletes have tested positive but claim that all they have taken was a cough mixture or other such product that can be bought over the counter.

Drug abuse is the ultimate in gamesmanship — taking something to increase performance and to increase the chance of winning. There is a range of performance-enhancing drugs that athletes may take. Most originated as genuine medical treatments, but their side effects have been used by athletes illegally to improve performance. The range and availability of these types of drug are constantly increasing, making control very difficult.

The huge increase in the rewards of winning has resulted in more temptation for athletes to take drugs. New drugs come onto the scene all the time and this makes it very difficult for organisations such as the International Olympic Medal Commission to keep ahead. New drugs are more sophisticated and harder to detect because they often mimic naturally occurring hormones and chemicals. One of the most highlighted of this new wave of drugs is **erythropoietin** (EPO). EPO is a hormone that stimulates bone marrow to produce more red blood cells. It is claimed by scientists to improve aerobic performance by up to 15%. Other scientists state that it can have serious side effects because at night the new red blood cells become viscous and the heart has to work harder to move the blood around the body. It has been estimated that 25 athletes have died from the effects of taking EPO.

The role of international bodies in combating cheating

Since 1967, when it established its Medical Commission, the IOC has taken the lead in attempting to prevent the use of drugs in sport. Each year, the IOC produces a list of banned drugs which athletes are tested for when they take part in the Olympic games; many other sport governing bodies use this list too. Bodies also try to foster sportsmanship by giving Fair Play Awards (FIFA awards one at every World Cup competition).

What the examiners will expect you to be able to do

- Discuss the reasons for, and types of, deviance in global sport.
- Explain how the increasing commercialisation of global sport affects its structure and ethic.

Commercialism and the media in global sport

Key points

- The difference between amateur and professional.
- The development of open sports.
- The role of television and the increasing Americanisation of global sport.
- Sponsorship and the idea of sports as a commodity.
- The win ethic vs. the recreational ethic.
- The relationship between international competition and friendship on an individual and group basis.

Background

The modern Olympic Games were set up in 1896. At this time, the International Olympic Committee stated that sports performers should not make a living or any form of profit from sport.

The games were encased in the 'Olympic ideal'. The emphasis was on the enjoyment of taking part, not winning (amateurism). However, the dramatic rise in performance and needs of the media have led to athletes having to train all year round. This means that they need to earn a living from sport (professionalism). In the 1980s, the Olympics became more open and the rules were altered so that both amateurs and professionals could take part, although the latter soon became dominant, as more and more sports became professional and the win ethic prevailed.

The presence of the media has turned global sport into a commodity that can be bought and sold. Television companies pay out large amounts of money for broadcasting rights for sporting events, and advertisers and sponsors back sport because of the exposure they will get in the media. Many sports have either been adapted to suit the needs of television or have changed structure to attract television coverage. Examples of this include the introduction of tie-breaks in tennis and time-outs in American football.

A so-called golden triangle of sport has been created — media coverage brings sponsors and advertising to a sport, which are then essential for a sport to remain viable. Companies sponsor sports mainly as a means of cheap advertising — a way of getting into the public's living room.

Open competition

Both amateurs and professionals can compete in open competition. In most global sports, performers can now receive funding from a wide range of sources to enable them to train full-time in order to be able to compete at that level. Increasing problems over the concept of 'shamateurism' during the early 1990s led to most sports adopting open rules. Shamateurism occurred when amateur athletes were accepting payment from various sources in return for competing.

Americanisation

Americanisation is the process by which American trends and attitudes are imposed on others at the expense of domestic culture. The influence of television is immense and most sports in the USA rely entirely on the money generated through television deals and advertising revenue. This also means that the 'win ethic' dominates sport; sponsors want to associate their products with successful teams.

Sponsorship

The benefits of sponsoring the Olympic Games were first recognised in Ancient Greece, when prominent citizens gave financial support to the organisation of the games in return for public recognition and appreciation.

Patriot Georgios Averof was a leading sponsor of the first modern Games in 1896. His funds helped to pay for the Olympic stadium. Other benefactors included a number of other Greek businessmen and the church.

Regular sponsorship began in 1912 at the Olympic Games held in the Swedish capital, Stockholm. In that year, ten Swedish companies gave money to acquire permits to take photographs and sell souvenirs.

In 1920, in Antwerp, the Belgians adopted a promotional strategy that proved to be most profitable. The official competition programme was filled with advertisements, to the point where the reader had to actually search to find details of the competitors and the events.

In 1924, in Paris, advertising hoardings made their first and last appearance inside the stadiums. Four years later, the commercial right to use the Olympic logo began to be extended to other sectors. Advertising returned to the games' programmes, but not inside the competition areas, as the IOC had decided that this did not fit in with the Olympic spirit and ideals.

Television made its first appearance in the Olympic stadium in Berlin in 1936. At the London Olympics in 1947, television rights were assigned for the first time.

As the cost of organising the Olympic Games continued to increase, the relationship between sponsors and the Olympic movement expanded. In 1984, the Los Angeles Olympic Games were marked by the beginning of an organised contribution by the sponsors to groups at the games and the IOC adopted an ambitious marketing policy. As part of this, the companies sponsoring the games were divided into three categories, with 34 companies signing contracts with the IOC as official sponsors, 64 companies acquiring the rights to supply the Olympics and another 65 being granted authority to use Olympic symbols. Each category had its own exclusive rights and, in most cases, the sponsors were large multinational businesses.

Television rights for the Los Angeles Olympics were bought by 156 countries, among which was Greece, and it was estimated that over 2.5 billion viewers watched the now global event.

For the Seoul Olympic Games in 1988, a highly developed marketing programme was created in cooperation with the IOC, the Organising Committee and various National Olympic Committees. It was decided to reduce dramatically the number of sponsors in order to increase the value of the rights, while the number of products and services linked with Games was limited.

At the Atlanta Olympics in 1996, all the expenses were covered by private funding, through television rights, sponsors and ticket sales. Television viewers were estimated to number 3.2 billion in a then record 214 nations and the number of tickets sold approached 11 million.

However, the example set by the Americans was not followed by the Australians in 2000. At the Sydney Olympics, 63% of the expenses were covered by sponsors and rights and the remainder by the Australian government. These games boasted 3.7 billion viewers in 220 countries. Four billion people watched the Athens Olympics in 2004, which was covered by 300 broadcast channels.

What the examiners will expect you to be able to do

- Track the historical development of 'open' sport.
- Explain the role of television and Americanisation in the funding of global games.
- Compare the win ethic with the recreational ethic.
- Discuss the main difference between amateur and professional sports performers.

Opportunity in global sport

Key points

- Individual differences (physiological, psychological and biomechanical) and their effect on access to sport.
- The influence of race, gender and religion on opportunity in global sport.
- Olympic and other sporting ideals evident in global games.
- Global sports as a means to break discrimination.
- Issues of stacking, centrality and sporting myths.

Influences on opportunity

Opportunity in sport is influenced by constraint. There are several factors that must be considered. In terms of athletic capability, people's **physiological**, **psychological** and **biomechanical** make-up will determine the opportunities available to them.

Sport can have both positive and negative influences on breaking discrimination. The global profile can have a positive influence, helping to promote sport among minority groups and to break down the barriers by creating role models. However, sport reflects the society in which it is played. If discrimination exists within a nation, then this is mirrored in sport. Sport also tends to reinforce the stereotypes and myths that are often linked to minority groups. Stereotypes and myths can become 'self-fulfilling prophecies' — even the people they discriminate against may come to believe they are valid and conform to the stereotypes by displaying the appointed characteristics and choosing the sports that fit them. In doing so, they are reinforcing the view of society.

Opportunity can be constrained by issues of **gender**, **race** and **religion**, which can seriously restrict access and opportunity in sport at all levels.

Gender

The increase in the number of women participants in most sports may lead you to believe that gender issues are no longer a factor in limiting opportunity. However, in some cultures, sometimes because of religion, it is still not accepted that women should compete in sports events. Global sport faces a dilemma with this issue. Should nations that do not bring female teams or competitors be excluded from events or should the hope be that their involvement will eventually break down these barriers?

The historical role of women in western society is seen as needing to conform to a set image, referred to as 'femininity'. Consequently, the amount and type of sport women play may be expected to adhere to this. There have been many myths about women and sport, though these have now been largely dismissed as inaccurate. Other problems concern time. Many women, because of the demands of work and family, tend to have much less leisure time than men and when they do have time, they are often exhausted. A lack of competitions/leagues makes participation and professionalism difficult for female sports performers.

Race

Some ethnic minority groups are discriminated against, which can seriously restrict access and opportunity in sport at both national and international levels. Often minority groups within a community are labelled as having certain body types, characteristics or traits. As a result, they can be steered into certain sports or positions and away from others. This concept is referred to as stereotyping.

THE HENLEY COLLEGE LIBRARY

Often there is a double effect within a culture, as the minority groups may also be lower income groups.

The Olympic ideal

The Olympic ideal states that the purpose of the games is to 'build a peaceful and better world by educating the youth of the world through sport, practised without discrimination of any kind and in the Olympic spirit, which requires mutual understanding, promoted by friendship, solidarity and fair play'.

The Olympic ideal also states that athletes should be free to participate in the Olympic Games irrespective of race, colour or creed.

Sportsmanship and gamesmanship

Sport relies on sportsmanship, i.e. people conforming to the written and unwritten rules. The idea of fair play means that opponents are treated as equals and, although the aim is to win, this should be done by adhering to the rules. A code of conduct has been developed in the sport through tradition. This includes shaking hands and congratulating the other team at the end of the game.

The alternative dynamic in sport is known as gamesmanship, in which any means possible are used to overcome the opponent. Here, the only aim is to win. For most people, this is not a question of breaking the rules but rather bending them to their own advantage.

Issues of stacking, centrality and sporting myths

There are a number of sociological theories linked to the issue of discrimination in sport. **Stacking** refers to the disproportionate concentration of ethnic minority players in certain positions in a sports team, which tends to be based on the stereotyped view that they are best suited to roles that require physical ability, rather than decision-making or communication skills. A linked theory is called **centrality** — the dominant role in a team is carried out by the dominant group in society — often WASPs (White Anglo-Saxon Protestants).

Stereotypes and sports myths are also societal variables that lead to discrimination.

What the examiners will expect you to be able to do

- Identify individual differences and their effects on access to sport.
- Explain physiological, psychological and mechanical differences.
- Explain the influence of race, gender and religion on opportunity in global sport.
- Explain the Olympic and other sporting ideals that are evident in global games.
- Discuss how global sports can act as a means to break discrimination, including the issues of stacking, centrality and sporting myths.

Effective essay writing

Section B of Unit 4 comprises synoptic questions. The term synoptic refers to an overview of knowledge. In order to answer any synoptic question, you should refer to a range of topic areas. The main theme for synoptic questions is 'global games' and you will need to refer to a range of examples from various global games in your answer.

The Unit 4 synoptic section reflects on the sociocultural units you have studied at AS and A2.

A good essay will:
- have a clear, recorded plan (which must be flexible and answer the question)
- be at least two sides in length and divided into paragraphs
- have an introduction that provides an overview of the essay content
- define terms
- work through the question in an identifiable order (e.g. chronologically, with examples in a logical order)
- refer to different global games and not just be a reproduction of an AS Olympic essay
- be analytical and challenge ideas with substantiated arguments
- have a conclusion that sums up the answer
- have answered the question

A poor essay will:
- contain the question written out again
- not have a plan
- be written in bullet points
- guess at facts, figures and dates
- have dates out of sequence
- reproduce or regurgitate a premeditated essay plan
- favour only one side of an argument rather than remaining neutral

In the exam

Read the questions *carefully* — at least twice — to ensure that you understand fully what each is asking. Plan your time and stick to your plan. Aim to spend at least 35 minutes writing your essay.

A typical plan structure
Paragraph 1: introduction — work through the question
Paragraph 2: definitions — cover the key terms in the question and bring in any other terms you are going to use
Paragraph 3: historical overview/scientific overview
Paragraph 4: examples/case study from global games
Paragraphs 5, 6 and 7: answer the question!
Paragraph 8: summary plus a personal statement of your own view on the subject

Questions
&
Answers

This section contains questions similar in style to those you can expect to see in your Unit 4 examination. The limited number of example questions here means that it is impossible to cover all the topics and all the question styles, but they should give you an idea of what to expect. The responses that are shown are real students' answers to the questions. In this paper you will answer two questions — one from Section A on a global culture and one essay from Section B.

There are several ways of using this Questions and Answers section.

- 'Hide' the answers to each question and try the question yourself. It needn't be a memory test — use your notes to see if you can actually make all the points you ought to make.
- Check your answers against the candidates' responses and make an estimate of the likely standard of your response to each question.
- Check your answers against the examiner's comments to see if you can appreciate where you might have lost marks.
- Check your answers against the terms used in the question — did you *explain* when you were asked to, or did you merely *describe*?

Examiner's comments

All the candidate responses are followed by examiner's comments. These are preceded by the icon 🖉 and indicate where credit is due. In the weaker answers, they also point out areas for improvement, specific problems and common errors such as lack of clarity, weak or non-existent development, irrelevance, misinterpretation of the question and mistaken meanings of terms.

1

Sport ethics in the USA

There are three main ethics that dominate both life and the sports scene in the USA:

- **Lombardian**
- **radical**
- **counter-culture**

**Define each of the above. Give an example of a sporting activity in the USA
that represents each ethic.**

(6 marks)

Total: 6 marks

■ ■ ■

Candidates' answers to Question 1

Candidate A

Lombardian means to win at all costs. In this ethic, winning is the only thing. All the four big professional sports (American football, baseball, basketball and ice hockey) represent this ethic.

Radical means winning is important, but not at all costs. Little League sports, such as Pee Wee baseball, represent this ethic.

Counter-culture means everyone takes part in the activity — not focusing on winning, but just for the sake of participating.

Candidate B

The Lombardian ethic states that 'winning isn't everything, it's the only thing'. American football is highly competitive; the Superbowl is basically a competition of survival of the fittest — in order to progress, you must win. The radical ethic is where winning and the means of winning are important. An example would be a golfer such as Tiger Woods, who wants to win the tournament and also wants to post a good score against the course. The counter-culture ethic is where people use the natural environment for their sporting activities. In this ethic, winning doesn't matter; taking part does. Trekking and camping are good examples.

ℯ This question requires candidates to work out how many points are needed to answer each part. Candidate A sets out the answer in a clear and logical way. It is easy to see that he has understood what the question is asking and has matched the answer structure to this. Candidate A scores well but does not gain full marks because an example of the counter-culture ethic is not given. He scores 5 out of the 6 marks available. Candidate B scores the maximum 6 marks. She has defined each ethic correctly and given an example of each. However, the answer is not as easy for the examiner to read.

Question 2

Extra-curricular sport in US schools and colleges

Extra-curricular sport in US schools and colleges is unique in its high status.
(a) Outline the provision for interschool/college sport and intramural sport in a
North American culture you have studied. (6 marks)
(b) Describe how the sports scholarship system links education and professional
sport in North America. (4 marks)

Total: 10 marks

■ ■ ■

Candidates' answers to Question 2

Candidate A

(a) Many people in the town will come to watch and support the local school or college. America is unique in the way that local communities pay to watch this level of sport. Games take place on a Friday night so that they can attract huge audiences. For those that cannot attend, the games are screened on local television channels. Booster clubs are set up by local businessmen to help raise money for the school or college team.

(b) Scholarships are what students strive for while at school. College football acts as the minor league for the NFL professional teams. While at college, all players aim to get into the draft in their final year. The draft is the system by which college players are selected to play in professional teams. Players who do not make the draft either give up or carry on playing only college football.

Candidate B

(a) The standards of sport in American colleges are high and the local community becomes involved with the team. There are booster clubs that help fund the college teams so that they can fly to away games and that ensure that the team gets new kit for every game. Also, the community will watch the local school or college football teams. This raises a considerable amount of money for the school. This is used to prepare the teams and to help fund and provide a wide range of other sports in the school or college. School and college football matches take place on Friday nights. Often people in the community will have Friday afternoon off work to prepare for the game. This encourages many students to become involved in sport at school and college. The best players will be offered scholarships that pay all their college fees.

(b) The scholarship system links professional sport and education because if people are good enough at a sport, they will receive a scholarship to attend college and play in the college team. They have to continue with an academic programme and need to keep their grades high enough to stay in college or they will be asked to leave and they will lose their scholarship. The way that the college leagues are structured and organised mirrors the professional leagues so that the college players get used to the style. This makes it easier for them to move up to the professional ranks. At the end of each college season the best college players from across the US are selected to go into the draft system. They are ranked on their ability and this determines their positions in the order of the draft. The worst professional team of the previous season gets the first pick of the best college players. This is the only route available to young Americans who want to make a career in professional sport.

e Both candidates appear to have a good grasp of this popular exam topic. They identify the main links between the education system and professional sport. Candidate A drops marks by not making enough points — examiners want you to match points to the marks allocated to each question. Neither candidate makes points about intramural sport in (a). Each scores only 4 marks. This may be because of a lack of knowledge or because this is mentioned at the end of a long paragraph. It is important that you keep stopping and checking that you have answered all parts of the questions set. Intramural sport means sport within a college in which faculty or social teams play in 'house' matches. It tends to happen after the college matches, which often means late at night. Candidate A scores 2 marks on part (b) for the explanation of the draft system. Candidate B scores maximum marks on part (b) — note the number of different points made. Overall, Candidate A scores 6 out of a possible 10 marks. Candidate B scores 8 marks.

Nurture of sporting talent in the USA

How does the draft system reflect America's claims of equality and of being the 'land of opportunity'?

(3 marks)

Total: 3 marks

■ ■ ■

Candidates' answers to Question 3

Candidate A

The American football draft system reflects America's claims of equality and of being the land of opportunity:

(1) The draft provides equality in two ways. First, every graduating college player is entered in the draft. This means that every player has an equal opportunity of being picked, depending on the scouting reports and the player's ability. Second, 'team equality' is determined by the league position of each team at the end of the season. The draft picks work in reverse order. Last year, the San Diego Chargers finished 32nd in the NFL leagues. Therefore, they were awarded the first pick of the draft, which they then traded for an existing professional player and a different first round pick. The New England Patriots won the Superbowl and finished first. Therefore, they had the last pick in the draft.

(2) The 'land of opportunity' is reflected in American football by the opportunity each player has to live the American Dream and become a professional player. This chance is open to all Americans, regardless of race or background — they simply have to work hard and develop their abilities. Also, the opportunity to try and equal out the teams through the draft pick means that at the start of each season all teams have an equal chance of winning the league.

Candidate B

The draft is a system that allows the teams lowest in the league to get first choice of the players who have been ranked in the college games and are looking for a professional contract. This is an attempt to even out the league at the start of each season. The richest clubs are not allowed to dominate the league by buying all the best players.

🖉 Both candidates make a good attempt at answering this question but do so using different styles. Candidate A covers most of the main points and does exactly what the question asks by making points that relate clearly to the terms 'equality' and 'land of opportunity'. He backs up these points with detailed and valid examples. This response scores the maximum 3 marks. Candidate B provides a much briefer answer but still makes valid points. However, it is harder to see exactly how these points relate to the two parts of the question, so the examiner has to do a little more work. She scores 2 marks.

Commercial issues in US sport

American sport is based on commercialism — profit often overtakes the more traditional sporting values. Using American football as an example, comment on this statement.

(4 marks)

Total: 4 marks

■ ■ ■

Candidates' answers to Question 4

Candidate A

- American football is based on commercialism. The sport was redesigned to suit television in the 1960s. There are many breaks in play to allow the television stations to show adverts.
- With permission from the league, team franchises move from city to city, depending on the size of the crowds at games and local area revenue.
- Stadiums have names such as 'Wrigley Field', which show a link to a commercial club sponsor. Teams, such as the Green Bay Packers, have names that highlight their commercial backers.
- The biggest piece of commercialism is gamesmanship, also known as the win-at-all-costs ethic. This approach has replaced the concept of sportsmanship. Winning puts you in the world's 'shop window', which will bring more sponsorship and more money. No company wants to associate its brand with a team that loses. Therefore, teams at the top of leagues always receive the most money in sponsorship deals.
- The richest franchise is that of the Dallas Cowboys, who have made $1 billion. The team was started as a commercial venture by the Washington Redskins to boost revenue. However, the Cowboys team proved so successful that it was awarded its own franchise.

Candidate B

American football is used as a business because money is such a big part of the game. For example, commercialism rules over the game so much that the media determine when games stop and start — to suit peak-time audiences and to allow as many adverts as possible to be shown.

Americans want to win everything in which they compete. They see second place as a place for losers. They see it as 'nice guys finish last' and because of this, American teams and athletes always put in 100% effort. American life is changing, with more emphasis being placed on the attitude that 'winner takes all'.

ℓ Both candidates make a good attempt at answering this question but do so using different styles. Candidate A covers most of the main points and does exactly what the question asks by matching each point to an example taken from American football. This 'bullet' style of answer is acceptable in this section of the paper, as long as it makes sense and is fully explained. Candidate B writes in a more traditional style. She makes several points but does not always link these to American football. Therefore, the question is not fully answered. The main focus of the question is to comment on and explain the statement: '…profit often overtakes the more traditional sporting values'. Neither candidate really answers this fully, although Candidate A does offer some relevant points. When commercial pressure becomes the driving force in sport, an attitude of win-at-all-costs develops. Here, success is essential for the continuing career of coaches and players, and unsporting practices such as drug taking, gamesmanship and deliberately harming opposition players may be seen as acceptable strategies. Candidate A scores 3 out of the 4 marks available. Candidate B scores 2 marks.

Colonial history of sport in Australia

Explain how the colonial history of Australian cultures is reflected in the structure and status of sport.

(4 marks)

Total: 4 marks

■ ■ ■

Candidates' answers to Question 5

Candidate A

- Sport gives a country such as Australia a shop window that allows it to gain world status.
- Australia had colonial links with the UK — sport followed the British flag.
- Sports from the UK were adapted to reflect the new culture, e.g. Aussie Rules football developed from rugby.
- Many sports in Australia are administered and structured in the same way as UK sports, e.g. clubs affiliated to national governing bodies.
- Australians invented the term 'test match' to compete against Britain as a way of checking their progress.

Candidate B

Australia adopted and adapted versions of British sports and these are now played in the country. They give Australians a sense of identity and a chance to acquire money and fame. Many Australian sports stars such as Harry Kewell now play sport in the UK where they can earn more money. Australia uses sport as a shop window to gain status from other countries. Winning gold medals puts Australia on the world map.

e The candidates use different styles to answer this question. Candidate A writes in a very concise style using bulleted sentences to make a number of good points. This approach can be an effective way of answering exam questions. However, you must remember to use bulleted sentences (*not* bullet points) and to ensure that your statements make sense. Candidate B uses a more continuous style. Both candidates score points for referring to the concept of shop window and the link to the UK. Candidate A goes on to give examples of these links and scores the maximum 4 marks. Candidate B makes more points about sport in the modern era, misreading the reference in the question to history. She scores 2 marks.

uestion 6

Structure of school sport in Australia

How does the structure of school sport and PE in Australia compare with that in the UK?

(5 marks)

Total: 5 marks

■ ■ ■

Candidates' answers to Question 6

Candidate A

In Australian schools, more time is allocated during the school timetable to PE and sport than in the UK. In the UK, students have to take up lunch-time and after-school periods to play sport. In both countries, PE is compulsory — all students have to do it. In Australia, every student makes it into a school team; in the UK, only the best do. More emphasis is given to PE in early years in Australia and PE and sport have more status and importance in Australian schools. The Australian government spends £40 per person per year on sport.

In UK primary schools, there is no specific lesson or teacher for PE. Generally, PE is seen as less important than, for example, maths or English.

Candidate B

PE and school sport in Australia	PE and school sport in the UK
School team sport is played during schooltime, i.e. during the school day.	Teams play and practise at after-school clubs and lunch-times in extra-curricular sessions.
Structured PE lessons are introduced in the primary school programme. Young children follow a fundamental motor skills programme.	Most students do not have proper PE lessons until secondary school. The UK does not have a fundamental motor skills programme.
PE is compulsory. All students must do at least 100 minutes of PE and 100 minutes of sport education per week. In some primary schools, there is a daily PE lesson.	It is advised that all students should do 2 hours of PE and sport per week. Most schools do not offer this because of the time needed for other subjects.
Schools run a sport education programme called SEPEP, which means that all Australian students have to play sport every week.	There is a limited sport education programme. Only students who play after school for school teams play sport. This may not occur every week.

e Neither answer scores maximum marks. The question asks the candidates to compare the structure of school sport and PE in Australia and the UK. The key here is to remember that to score a point you have to give both parts of the comparison. Therefore, to score 5 marks on this question you have to make ten points — five for each country, but linked together. Candidate B answers in table form. This is an effective way of answering questions that ask for comparison because it reminds you to compare points. You have to remember that what you write in each box must make sense. Candidate B scores well here, giving a detailed answer with named examples. However, only four (correct) comparisons are made and, therefore, only 4 of the 5 marks available are gained. Candidate A answers in a different style that works to some extent. However, towards the end of the answer the comparison becomes harder to see. Candidate A therefore only scores 3 out of 5 marks as he has repeated the point about differences in primary school PE. Remember that in a comparison question, you don't just have to look for differences — you can also gain marks for stating similarities.

Global sport and nationalism

Using examples from the cultures you have studied, discuss how sporting success in global games can benefit a country both internally and externally. (50 marks)

Total: 50 marks

■ ■ ■

Candidates' answers to Question 7

Candidate A

Plan

(1) Define key terms in question
(2) Explain what question is looking for
(3) Historical overview of sports success in global games
(4) Examples of global games and their effects on nations
(5) Answer question directly, referring to internal and external effects
(6) Conclusion

Essay

The cultures that I have studied are Australia and the USA. These are two very different cultures and success in sport affects them in different ways. Global games are events that work on a global scale, which involve many countries both taking part and spectating. Internal benefits include financial benefits, children participating and national pride. External benefits include attracting the attention and respect of the world.

For a long time, global games have been used by countries as a shop window. Sporting success is used as a measure of a country's success. If a small nation wins a lot of medals, it shows that it is performing out of its league. Therefore, it shows that it is using an effective method of gaining shop-window success. However, if a large nation has little success, it shows that it has an ineffective method. People tend to believe that if a country is good at sport, then it is a strong country. Sport is used as a window into that country — it is used to attract attention.

Two examples of global games that are very influential are the Olympics and the FIFA World Cup.

The first culture that I studied — Australia — has used sport as a way of attracting world attention. It is a country with a small population, yet in major world games such as the Olympics it often comes in the top five. This is a magnificent achievement for a country with such a small population that should, in theory, be way down the medal tables. Australia is out on its own away from other NATO countries and very near China, which could invade. Bringing Australia into the international spotlight helps improve national security.

On the other hand, America uses global games as a way to prove that it is the strongest country in the world. America goes to the Olympics expecting to come out

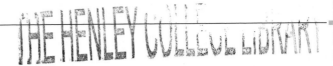

THE HENLEY COLLEGE LIBRARY

on top of the medal tables. When this happens, it is a way for Americans to boast that they belong to the greatest country on Earth. They believe that winning global sporting events proves this.

Internally, both countries use success as a way of improving child participation in sport within the country. If children see people winning global events, then participation in that sport will increase. For example, when England won the Rugby World Cup the number of children playing rugby went up ten-fold. It is so influential that it can also improve people's pride in their country. The population of a top sporting nation will be prouder than that of a poor sporting nation.

In conclusion, sport is a very important part of global standing. Countries use sport as a way of attracting attention and showing how good they are. Success in sport increases national pride and children's participation. All in all, sporting success leads to good things for the countries involved.

Candidate B

Plan

(1) Introduction

(2) Explain success linked to financial and other benefits for a country

(3) Examples: e.g. Rugby World Cup

(4) Include internal and external benefits, such as trade agreements

(5) Explain the role of sponsors

(6) Conclusion

Essay

In this essay, I will outline the benefits a country can accrue from achieving success in global games. I will attempt to give examples from the cultures I have studied in section A of this unit. The key focus of the essay will be the use of sport as a shop window for nations.

The success of a country in global sports competitions can bring important economic benefits. These constitute an internal benefit to the country. The money can be used to boost the infrastructure of the country, which could include improving roads. The boost to the economy could also be used to improve the nation's health services and to attract foreign investment. A successful sports nation creates a good image.

Internal benefits also include improving the nation's sporting facilities. An example of this is seen in Kenya. One of Kenya's most successful athletes, Wilson Kipketer, has reinvested some of the money he earned from sports success by setting up four national sports centres, with the aim of encouraging the next generation of Olympic champions.

Sporting success can help the various cultural groups within a nation. There is also some evidence that it may help lower crime rates and antisocial behaviour. In 1995, South Africa hosted the Rugby World Cup. It was the first time the country had been allowed to host a major event since the abolition of apartheid. Hosting the games, and the fact that South Africa won the final, had a huge impact on the nation, encouraging racial harmony and having a positive effect on reducing crime rates in South African cities.

Another benefit that can result is an improved participation rate among the population. Successful sports stars are used as role models and can encourage more people to take up sport or to improve their fitness. With more people participating in sport, the sports pyramid predicts that there should be a corresponding rise in sporting talent.

A good example of this benefit is in Australia, where global sports success has led to huge participation rates. In the census taken just after the Sydney Olympics, Australia recorded a 90% participation rate amongst its population. This must have a link with hosting such a successful Olympic Games.

This effect can also be seen in Morocco, where success in global sport has had a knock-on effect upon participation. The 1500 m runner Hicham El Guerrouj is one of the most successful middle-distance runners of the last decade and there are now many more young Moroccans attempting to emulate their hero. Sporting heroes can have a huge effect on the positive self-esteem of the people, developing a feeling of pride and inspiring the belief that they can compete with the best in the world.

An increase in participation can also have a positive impact on the economy of a country, with more jobs being created and unemployment being reduced. These jobs are created because of the increase in the need for sports facilities, equipment and clothing. As the economy improves, this can improve the quality of life for the whole country.

Internal and external benefits are closely linked. Many internal benefits are created as a result of the external benefits that come from success in global games. As mentioned in the introductory paragraph, many countries use sport as a shop window, and success in global sports events can lead to a positive international image. This has many benefits, such as increasing the international profile of a country and bringing political and commercial status. Emergent cultures, such as Kenya and Namibia, may use sport to gain world status.

Other external benefits arising from sports success include the setting up of trade agreements between countries. These bolster trade and increase wealth. An example of this is the England soccer team playing fixtures against Gulf States. This has helped the UK government gain contracts to build fighter planes. Another example is the way that many US companies, such as Nike, use Kenyan athletes and Kenyan workers to promote and produce their products.

External benefits also include enticing big-name sponsors for teams and bringing in revenue when television networks — often from other countries — pay large amounts of money to buy the exclusive rights to screen global sports competitions. This is particularly true for events such as the Olympics and the football World Cup.

Success can also lead to a country being entered into more competitions. For example, Italy's success in the 1995 Rugby World Cup led to an invitation to join the renamed European Six Nations Rugby Championships.

In conclusion, I have highlighted the many benefits that success in global games can bring. These benefits can be internal to a country and its population and external (in terms of the profile of the country). The key internal benefits of global sports success are financial — an improved economy — and a positive effect on sports participation. Many countries and governments around the world have realised the power that sports success can bring and are now developing systems for nurturing elite talent, in order to ensure future success. Perhaps this is something we in the UK are yet to grasp fully. If we are not careful, we may be left behind — even emerging countries are developing sophisticated sports institutes to help support their elite athletes. I think that the huge global audiences that now watch major events and the commercial opportunities this brings are probably the main reasons for this interest in sports success.

e Candidate A starts off well, with a good introduction. However, the answer soon runs out of steam. The candidate does not stick to the plan. For example, no real explanation of the rule of the soccer world cup is given, yet it is stated in the third paragraph that this will be used as a main case study in his answer. The candidate makes a number of valid points but does not back them up with facts or figures. The examples used are a little vague and not always fully related to the topic. This answer would score 24 marks out of a possible 50. Candidate B produces a detailed answer in terms of quantity and the number of points and global examples given. This answer is well structured and moves along well, with paragraphs of good length and a clear opening and conclusion. The candidate gives an impression of analysis, debating and challenging many of the related issues. Points made are backed up with reference to a game or culture. Some technical terms are given, though they are not always defined or explained. She finishes off the answer with some personal and original thoughts — always a good idea in the higher-mark questions. Candidate B scores 40 marks.

Question 8

Sports excellence in global sport

Discuss how the East European model of sports excellence is now being adopted by countries around the globe in their pursuit of global sporting success. (50 marks)

Total: 50 marks

■ ■ ■

Candidates' answers to Question 8

Candidate A

Plan

(1) Introduction

(2) Keywords: excellence, shop window of sports success

(3) Historical overview: move from recreational ethic to win ethic

(4) Example: East Germany

(5) Answer the question: why choose an elite system — advantages and disadvantages

(6) Answer the question: adoption — Australia 1976 failure/UKSI/French — INSEP

(7) Answer the question: adaptation — sport reflects society; use comparative study and reform own system

(8) Summary and personal statement

Essay

In the pursuit of global excellence through sport, countries are developing their own programmes for nurturing talent. In answering this question, I will first give a historical overview and then use examples of sports excellence to relate this subject to other global cultures. I will then explain why elite systems are used and how countries adopt and adapt these systems to fit their own societies. I shall conclude with my personal opinions.

In 1896, Baron de Coubertin revived the Olympic Games in an attempt to bring countries together to compete in a healthy and friendly atmosphere. He hoped that this might help prevent war and bring about international friendship, free from political issues. Sportsmanship was the key to these early games and this is why, even to this day, athletes take the Olympic oath. However, over the years, the Olympic Games and other international competitions have shifted from the recreational ethic towards Vince Lombardi's ideal of the 'win ethic'. Achievement-orientated, reward-based behaviour has led to more athletes striving for success.

Elitism has taken over the ideal of optimal performance in an attempt to nurture more champions. The East German model exemplifies the elitist approach to performance. With a population of only 16 million, East Germany managed to achieve international status by selecting and developing athletes at a young age, often before the age of six.

When it comes to pursuing sports as a shop window to portray global success, why do countries choose an elite system? The philosophy of 'pick the best, ignore the rest' is used at the expense of the remainder of the population. A political aspect of this system is that short-term results can be achieved with an efficient use of limited funds. However, the disadvantage of this ideal is that it promotes the win ethic and puts no emphasis on participation. As rewards become greater, sporting ethics go out of the window and problems such as deviance occur.

In 1976, after its Olympic failure, Australia adopted the East German model of sporting excellence. However, Australia has also been successful in the upkeep of grass-roots participation in sport. A well-balanced pyramid of participation has been developed, with, according to the 2000 census, 90% of the population of all ages being actively involved in sport. Also, Australia often finishes in the top three in international sports competitions. Other countries have adopted the East German model too. In the UK, a United Kingdom Institute of Sport network has been developed and in France the INSEP (Institut National du Sport et de l'Education Physique) has been introduced.

Although many nations have adopted the East German model for excellence, copying it won't work for all countries. Because sport reflects society, countries have to adapt this model to suit them. Although the UK has a slight emphasis on elitism with the recently established World Class Programme, more funding is placed within the public sector by the National Lottery.

In conclusion, I believe that Australia, although it has a small population, has achieved a well-balanced system of sporting excellence which, since the 1976 Montreal Olympic failure, has gradually made Australia into a shop window for sport. In many countries today, for example China and the USA, the win ethic has taken over the ideal that Baron de Coubertin wanted to achieve. Sport has been driven into political issues and commercial interests. No wonder the USA is the most obese nation. Why would people want to play sport if they don't want to go professional? There is no opportunity for the people who just want an active lifestyle that is enjoyable. If global success is the pursuit of all countries, then in the years to come the grass-roots of sport are going to be ruined. The money gained through global success as a shop window will soon have to pay for the healthcare of the rest of the population, as a result of the absence of promotion of physical exercise in general amateur terms.

Candidate B

Plan

(1) Introduction
(2) Definitions: East German sports model, talent identification, sports schools, high-level coaching, advanced scientific support
(3) Historical overview: recreational ethic to win ethic; concept of elitism vs. optimum performance
(4) The East German sports model as a case study
(5) Why East Germany adopted an elite sports model: new country after war, boost global identification, sport used as a shop window
(6) Advantages and disadvantages of an elitist system: win-at-all-costs pushing sports ethics to limit, commercial factors

question

(7) Adaptation: I don't think this question is right — most countries have changed the model to suit their own particular cultures and societies; sport reflects the culture in which it is played

(8) Personal statement conclusion: success? Whether or not the UK should go for this — committing money to such a small group of people

Essay

In answering this question, I will first give an overview of excellence in global sport. By using examples, I will identify the reasons why countries have adopted the East German model of sports excellence. In my conclusion, I will review whether countries have adopted or adapted the model and put forward my own opinions.

Excellence is an important current global issue. When defining excellence, we have to look at two concepts that are involved — elitism and optimum performance. Elitism is the emphasis on only a few performers. The best performers are identified and developed and the rest of the population is ignored. In contrast to elitism, optimum performance asserts that sporting excellence should be the target of every individual. The development of excellence includes selecting talent, developing talent and providing support. This is carried out in a number of different ways. Some countries have sports schools. Young people are sometimes sent to a residential facility that also provides full-time education. Others attend sports academies, which are establishments that have the primary aim of developing performance to the highest level.

To pursue excellence, various sporting models have been adapted. One example is the East European model, which includes identification of talent at an early age, enrolment in sports schools, high-level coaching and advanced scientific support. This model has been widely copied throughout the world.

Across the globe, sporting success is high on governments' agendas. During the course of the twentieth century, sport has moved from the recreational ethic — it is the taking part that counts, not winning — to the win ethic — performers strive to win, no matter what the cost. Globally, in the pursuit of excellence, countries have used ideas from other countries. The East European model of sporting excellence originated in East Germany. It came about in the 1960s to boost its communist system. The shop window (a term used to describe a market place in which a nation displays its sporting talent and in doing so gains publicity for its cultural, economic and political infrastructure) was the main objective of the Soviet Union. However, in this case it was the political system that was on show.

East Germany needed a successful sporting model because it was a new country after the war and needed to boost its global identity through the use of the shop window. The Eastern bloc model included selection of talent through the screening of young people for sporting potential and talent development, which included a highly structured system of specialist sports schools. The sports science studied included biomechanics, nutrition, sports physiology, sports psychology, physiotherapy and rehabilitation, which all contributed to success. Much of the Eastern bloc success has been attributed to the widespread use of drugs, although this alone could not account for the degree and rate of success. Some success must be attributable to the fact that the Eastern bloc countries had the best facilities, coaches and support available.

The success of the East European model has meant that, in their pursuit of excellence, many countries have adapted it. The UK is an example of such a country. The United Kingdom Institute of Sport is a network of national sports centres across the country that includes Lilleshall Hall in Shropshire, the home of the National Sports Injuries Clinic. Techniques used in the East European model have been adopted here.

Looking back to the question asked, I think that the statement lacks some truth because in the global pursuit of excellence countries have not merely adopted the East European model; they have used it as a starting point and adapted it. I think this because sport reflects the society in which it is played and our society in the UK is not identical to that of the former East Germany. Each society has its individual differences. As stated before, due to East Germany's desperation to win, drugs were sometimes taken to gain unfair advantage. However, the UK adapted the East European model, because we do not believe in cheating.

The USA is another example of a country that has adapted, not adopted, the East European model. It has adapted the model by the introduction of the win ethic and commercial and financial input, as sport is now seen as a business. The superpower has its own domestic world champions.

The East European model of sports excellence has influenced countries, which have then adapted it to suit their societies. I believe that with the growing input of more money into sport, the number of talented performers is going to increase.

e Candidate A sets out a very thorough plan that is not quite matched in the answer. His answer gives a good overview of the issue and the structure is clear and easy to follow. Some examples are given, but these are not developed in any detail. For instance, the example of the former East Germany does not actually explain how that country produced elite performers. The use of sports institutes and early selection could have been included. The candidate becomes rather bogged down in the argument about elite sport vs. grass roots participation. Although this is a valid point, it is not really what the question asks for. Candidate A scores 22 out of the 50 marks available. Candidate B sets out a thorough plan and sticks to it fairly well. This answer contains a lot of detail and makes reference to a range of cultural examples. She adheres to the question set, although several bland statements are made and the counterargument set out in the plan is not really developed. For example, she suggests that the USA has adapted an East German model, but does not say how, or that this would be a major cultural 'swing' as the USA has a long history of being anti-communist. However, Candidate B does score 29 out of 50 marks, as a comprehensive answer has been produced containing points relating to four separate countries, and a reference to a range of sports science disciplines.

Deviance and fair play

'Professional sport demands that winning is the top priority — in the harsh business world of modern sport, success in sport equals commercial success.'

Discuss whether the concepts of fair play and sportsmanship still exist in the global games of the twenty-first century. (50 marks)

Total: 50 marks

■ ■ ■

Candidates' answers to Question 9

Candidate A

Plan

(1) Define key words

(2) Historical overview

(3) Case studies

(4) Answer question directly

(5) Personal statement on issues of fair play and sportsmanship

Essay

Sportsmanship is defined as the intention to compete within the framework and intended spirit of the rules. The alternative sporting ethic is gamesmanship. This is the intention to compete to the limit allowed by the rules, and beyond, if that is achievable without penalty. Professional athletes all want to win because winning gains respect for them as individuals and for their clubs or countries. Winning can result in extrinsic rewards, such as money or trophies.

As society has changed over the years, so has sport. This is because sports reflect society. In the nineteenth century, the recreational ethic was supported. This ethic states that taking part in sport is all that matters. In the twenty-first century, this has changed to the win ethic. This states that winning is all that counts and that we should win at all costs. The recreational ethic is supported by the people who love sport for intrinsic reasons, whereas the win ethic is supported by people who want the extrinsic benefits, such as money. John McEnroe epitomised the idea that 'you get away with what you can'. The Americans have moved towards the win ethic because money brings so much more drive to sport. This supports the American Dream that through sport a person can go from rags to riches. Because of the huge extrinsic rewards available to athletes in the USA, sports stars become millionaires.

Over time, there have been changes in sport. For example, we see more deviance. However, many say that cheating makes sport exciting and attracts larger audiences, therefore generating more money and extrinsic rewards for the performers. It is also debatable whether there really is more cheating and deviance in sport in the twenty-first century. Perhaps the wall-to-wall presence of television cameras just means that it is much easier for us to see examples of cheating.

Fair play does still exist. For example, in the FIFA World Cup, when Wayne Rooney was injured in the game against Portugal, the goalkeeper kicked the ball into touch so that Rooney could receive attention. In an attempt to promote sportsmanship and fair play, FIFA also presents fair play awards to teams in all the major soccer competitions.

Many morals will be put to the test as sport progresses through the twenty-first century. Some people believe it is better to win honourably rather than by cheating, whereas others believe that 'nice guys finish last' and that winning is the most important thing. Global sports show that fair play and sportsmanship, but also gamesmanship, still exist. For example, there was an incident in the FIFA World Cup in which Rivaldo pretended to be injured, resulting in another player being given a yellow card.

Candidate B

Plan

(1) Definitions of key words in the question
(2) Background overview of what has happened in the last two centuries of sports development
(3) Arguments and examples debating whether sportsmanship and fair play still exist
(4) Conclusion and personal judgement on the issue of deviance in sport in the future

Essay

The key word in this question is sportsmanship. This is to do with fair play and the idea that it is the taking part that counts. For example, on handling the ball in football a true sportsman would own up. Gamesmanship means the opposite of sportsmanship — it is not the taking part that counts, it is winning at all costs. Winning at all costs means just that, no matter if this involves taking drugs or fixing matches. In the USA, winning is everything. Americanisation has been brought over to the UK and Europe. Taking drugs does not seem to be an issue in the USA, as the present revelations about the widespread use of drugs in baseball suggest. It is possible to log onto the internet and purchase drugs such as nandrolone and EPO at the touch of a button. The reason for this apparent readiness to cheat is the prizes and prize money available.

In early sport, the recreation ethic was prevalent because people played for the love of the game and were not bothered about winning and money. However, over the years, this has evolved into the win ethic — performers will do whatever it takes to win so that they can receive a lot of money. This has become the only reason to play sport — to win money.

An example of sportsmanship in global games occurred in the 2004 World Cup finals when Wayne Rooney was injured in the match against Portugal and the goalkeeper, Ricardo, put the ball out of play so that Rooney could receive treatment. An example of gamesmanship and cheating occurred when Brazil played Turkey in the World Cup. A Turkish player kicked the ball at Rivaldo's shin and he fell down clutching his face, i.e. indicating that he had been hit in the face.

It can be argued that fair play and sportsmanship still exist in global games because in the football World Cup, when a player is injured and the opposition put the ball out

of play, the injured player gets up and gives the ball back to the opposition. This is sportsmanship. It is not written down in the laws of the game that the ball has to be thrown out of play. It happens because of the nature and fair play of the teams.

It can also be argued that sportsmanship does not exist in global games. People want to win for their country and gain accolades for themselves so much that sometimes sportsmen will try to obtain drugs that cannot be found when tested, so they will always cheat to win.

Overall, there are many positives and negatives. The quote 'nice guys finish last' means that if you don't cheat, then you won't win. However, in the World Cup, a fair play award is presented to the team that commits the fewest fouls and obtains the fewest yellow and red cards.

I think that both sportsmanship and gamesmanship will always occur in sport. It depends on the nature of the teams and athletes — whether there is the desire to win on the big stage or whether they would rather lose honourably and not cheat. The future of fair play will go on forever. Even in tennis, if players think the ball is in, they will say so, rather than cheat.

e Candidate A produces a sharp and concise answer that moves well through the question. A number of valid points are made that all relate to the question set. Both sides of the argument are given and a number of quotes and phrases are used to bulk out the points. However, the answer ends rather abruptly and does not really live up to the plan outlined at the start. The major weakness is a lack of practical examples and case studies to back up the points made. The candidate only starts to develop these at the end of the essay. Candidate A scores 30 out of the 50 marks available. Candidate B's answer contains a range of practical examples, indicating a sound understanding of this issue. The answer moves along well, though sometimes skirts over some of the points — a little more explanation is required in places. For example, the fifth paragraph introduces the problems of drugs in sport, but gives no real explanation of the issue, and makes no reference to any specific examples. Candidate B scores 26 marks.

Opportunity in global games

'Women have but one task — that of crowning the winner with garlands.'

(Baron de Coubertin, 1896)

In the light of this statement, comment on the changing role of women within global games. (50 marks)

Total: 50 marks

■ ■ ■

Candidates' answers to Question 10

Candidate A

Plan

(1) Brief historical overview of the role of women in the Olympics and other global games

(2) Examples of women in sport and how they have taken part in the Olympics

(3) Changing role from original Olympics to the modern games

(4) Review of women's role in global games

Essay

In answering this question, I will give a brief historical overview of the role of women in the Olympics and other global games. I shall highlight examples of women in sport and explain their participation in the Olympics. I will concentrate specifically on how the role of women has changed from the original to the modern-day Olympic games.

The statement by Baron de Coubertin means that he believed that women should not take part in the events in the Olympics — he thought it should be a men-only event. This comment was made at the start of the modern Olympic Games, which were founded by de Coubertin and reflected the general views held in most countries at the end of the nineteenth century. However, the role of women in global sport has changed. Women now play a much bigger role in most sports.

During the first modern Olympic Games held in 1896, there was only one female athlete. She was forbidden to take part in the men's marathon but completed the course on her own the following day. She had to finish her race outside the stadium because she was not allowed to enter. The officials could not remember her name, so called her Melpomene, which was the name of the ancient Greek muse of tragedy. Before this date, women did not take part in sport generally and played little part in global games such as the Olympics.

In 1900, the new century was celebrated with the World Exhibition. The Olympic Games took place at the same time, so were considered to be part of the celebrations. The International Olympic Committee had little influence on the games because they merged with the celebrations. This meant that women were able to take part. Events in which women participated included tennis, golf and yachting.

Charlotte Cooper, a tennis player from Great Britain, became the first woman to win an Olympic gold medal. It is interesting to note that women's golf and tennis remain high-profile global sports for women. Events such as the grand-slam tennis competitions and the Solheim Cup in golf are important global games.

Women gradually began to take part in more events over the next few Olympic Games. At the start of the twentieth century, these events included archery and gymnastics — sports that still reflected the feminine characteristics that society believed women should portray. Women held a number of demonstrations during the games because they believed that they should be allowed to compete in more events and match the men. In the 1920s, women, led by the French lady Alice Milliat, set up their own international women's games, reflecting this frustration. The British women's Olympic team boycotted the Olympic Games in 1928 because they wanted to compete in more events.

The pressure of an alternative games for women did finally persuade the IOC and other international sports bodies to take women's sport more seriously. In 1956, the Olympic oath at the opening ceremony was read by a female athlete and in 1968 another female athlete lit the Olympic flame, something repeated by Kathy Freeman at the Sydney Olympics in 2000. By the 1996 Olympic Games in Atlanta, there were 23 different sports for women and a further six at the winter Olympics in 1998, including, for the first time, curling and ice hockey.

The first pentathlon for women was held at the Sydney Olympics. It is facts such as this that allow me to conclude that women are now taking a much bigger role in global sport. Their role has changed from initially not being allowed to take part in any global games, to over 100 years later being able to compete in over 23 sports at the Olympics. This shows what an effect women's campaigning has had, because they are now being treated in the way they want.

Candidate B

Plan

(1) Historical overview of women in global sport
(2) Identify why there has been an increase in the number of female participants in global games such as the Olympics
(3) Review current role of women in global games
(4) Suggest where issue may go in the near future

Essay

In order to answer this question, I will give a short historical overview of the issue of women in global sport. I will identify why there has been an increase in the number of female participants in global games. I will then review the current role of women in global games and suggest where I think the issue may go in the near future.

The first modern Olympics were held in Athens in 1896. They were founded by Baron Pierre de Coubertin. De Coubertin had studied the ancient Olympic Games, but most of his inspiration came from the sports competitions held in English public schools during the nineteenth century. In the ancient games, women were forbidden to take part and married women could not even spectate. The public schools of England were exclusively male and this gender bias was to be reflected in the early global games set up at the start of the twentieth century.

When the Olympic Games were revived in 1896, Baron de Coubertin did not agree with women's participation in the games. It was not until the games of the twentieth century that women began to participate properly.

In 1908, there were 36 women competitors in figure skating and tennis events. This was a minute number compared with how many men took part, but it was a breakthrough for women. In 1968, Norma Enriqueta Basilio was the first woman to light the Olympic flame. In 1981, there was the first female member of the International Olympic Committee (IOC).

When Baron de Coubertin reinvented the Olympic Games, he discriminated against women. He stopped them from taking part and the female population had to prove they were physically able to compete. However, sporting myths discouraged women from participating in some events. For example, it was believed that taking part in hurdles could damage women internally. These myths are no longer believed and women are now empowered to take part.

There are also stereotypical views that women should be feminine and stay at home to be housewives. However, these views are part of the past and a large number of women now take part in some form of physical activity and it is seen as natural to do so.

There has been a large increase in the number of sports that are offered to women on a global scale — for example, football and rugby are no longer seen as male-only sports. This has led to the female population being able to participate in a wide range of sports. Women can now play at world level in many events.

Many women have become sport enthusiasts and the only things that are really holding them back are the constraints of family and work. Men are no longer portrayed as the only gender able enough to play sport. Women are sometimes better than men in events such as endurance running and swimming. For example, the current records for swimming the English Channel and the Thames are held by female swimmers.

In conclusion, women's development in sport has reflected their increasing status in the wider society. As stated at the start of this essay, sport reflects the society in which it is played. There are still issues in terms of the number of events available, and men continue to outnumber women at competitions such as the Olympics. There is also still an imbalance in the role of women in decision making and administration — there are not many women on the IOC. Nonetheless, global sport today is in a much better position than was the case at the end of the nineteenth century. Organisations such as the International Olympic Committee have now committed to increase the number of women officials and senior members, and this may eventually lead to a more equal view of global sport.

🖉 Both candidates have written a good opening paragraph. They have tended to use examples from the Olympics. These are valid, but it is expected that candidates will use examples from a range of global sports competitions. To some extent, Candidate A

does this, which improves his score. He starts off developing a sound answer but appears to run out of steam near the end. This could be because he ran out of time — the last few paragraphs do appear rushed. In the exam, you only have about 35–40 minutes to answer an essay question, so it is important to use the time efficiently. Candidate A scores 28 out of the 50 marks available. Candidate B's answer is more structured and balanced, and ends with a neat conclusion. A number of valid points are made, but the answer is let down by a lack of variation in the examples used. Candidate B scores 32 marks.